That's Not Who I Am

I Know Better Than That

Cheryl W. Spooner

WESTBOW
PRESS®
A DIVISION OF THOMAS NELSON
& ZONDERVAN

WestBow Press books may be ordered through booksellers or by contacting:

WestBow Press
A Division of Thomas Nelson & Zondervan
1663 Liberty Drive
Bloomington, IN 47403
www.westbowpress.com
844-714-3454

ISBN: 978-1-6642-9386-1 (sc)
ISBN: 978-1-6642-9387-8 (e)

Library of Congress Control Number: 2023903763

Print information available on the last page.

WestBow Press rev. date: 05/02/2023

This journal is dedicated to my mother, Julia, who gave everything for her children.
To my husband, children and grandchildren, I love you so dearly.
To my dear siblings who have taught me a lot about life.

Contents

Introduction

That's Not Who I Am

Take a look inside of yourself. What do you see? Your heart reveals who you are if you are willing to accept what you see. Being transparent is a great method to incorporate so you can be truthful to yourself. We should use transparency to see where there is a need for true change. We should look intently within to see how we can better ourselves. As you take an honest look, you may find areas you want to improve upon or change. We will see the truth about ourselves as we take off the lens that tends to blind us to who we really are.

That's Not Who I Am is a personal workbook that will help you see yourself for who you really are, as your own personal truth is declared. You will be able to see where there is a need for productive change or improvement. This tool will help you rethink how you want to live your life. This teaching tool is for children, adults, teachers, school personnel, professionals, clergy, community leaders, entrepreneurs, families, and anyone with a desire to make positive change happen in their lives.

This workbook is for those who are often ashamed of their behaviors and feel guilt and remorse afterward when they think, *That's not who I am.* This self-help workbook approach is for those who want to revisit who they are using a technique that is private and personal. *That's Not Who I Am* is for those who are not afraid to see themselves for who they really are. *That's Not Who I Am* is for the open-minded individual who has the desire and courage to work to develop skills that will eliminate weak areas and behaviors that are not conducive to making our homes, schools, and communities better places to live.

That's Not Who I Am highlights how to work to embrace and build on finding the positive strengths within. *That's Not Who I Am* encourages you to answer questions by writing down your thoughts, or journaling how to work on yourself to become all you were made to be.

That's Not Who I Am is a self-esteem booster. In utilizing this workbook, there is the possibility to make life-changing decisions that will increase your self-esteem. As you begin to explore untapped areas of your emotions, you will feel invited to question yourself about how to bring out the best you. The philosophy of *That's Not Who I Am* is not a new concept but it is a concept that needs to be revisited, re-explored, and revitalized in the minds and hearts of interested individuals. Some actions or behaviors have negative connotations and project wrong ideas about who you are. Some will say, "I don't care what people say about me." Is this a true statement? Realization that an understanding of oneself, one's character, and one's true identity is important to succeed in life.

Finding your fit, your expectations of yourself, and how you want others to perceive you is imperative. Have you ever been directed the wrong way and followed that wrong path? Have you been in a family or environment that taught wrong behaviors or allowed and permitted falsehoods? Have you lived a life of being misunderstood? Have you repeatedly been lied to, which led you to act out inappropriately? What was your response?

Have you been described as someone your peers did not like? Have you felt ashamed by your actions or behaviors? Did you have regrets afterwards? Did you feel terrible remorse? Were you ever excluded or felt excluded because you were labeled wrongly or negatively? Are you acting the opposite of who you are or desire to be? Do you feel uncomfortable in your own skin? Do you desire to change lifestyle patterns that produce negative outcomes? Are you afraid to embrace who you really are? Do you fear the result of your findings? Do you think negative behaviors, such as fighting or degrading others, make you feel secure? Do you have peace within yourself? Have you tapped into your heart to determine who you are?

That's Not Who I Am may be the tool you need to help you begin the journey to become the true you. *That's Not Who I Am* helps one to get in tune with oneself, and empowers one to make change happen for a productive lifestyle. Age is not a factor. It does not matter what age a person is. It's never too early or too late to improve yourself. It's an adventure to explore you.

Sometimes, it's difficult for us to accept what we see. It can be challenging to acknowledge our shortcomings. We can find it easy to blame others. But with grit and hard work, we can better ourselves and the world around us by taking a look at ourselves, the good, the bad and the ugly.

Just as there are several stages in the metamorphosis from a caterpillar to a butterfly, such is the journey for individual self-change. The time involved to burst forth into that transformed state of being may be short or long depending on the process. This butterfly concept is the essence of *That's Not Who I Am.*

That's Not Who I Am
Self–Inventory Interview Questionnaire Instructions
A personal reflection/journal/diary

This questionnaire is designed to take you on a journey with yourself. These thought provoking questions will help you take the time to think about yourself and your life as you answer truthfully about your life. By taking this time for yourself, you will evaluate your thoughts and your thought processes to determine if this is who you are and who you want to be. This personal self-assessment is valuable to understanding who you are, what is missing, and what needs to be incorporated into your life for complete satisfaction with self. This self-analysis will help you decide how you want to make positive change because positive change can come about—if you want it to.

The apostle Paul, in the Book of Romans, shared the following thought: "I have the desire to do what is good, but I cannot carry it out. For I do not do the good I want to do, but the evil I do not want to do this I keep on doing" (Romans 7:18–19). This passage, explains the core of the *That's Not Who I Am* perception. This is the challenge of our lives: to do good and not bad. We can agree to disagree on some issues, but let us agree to make a concerted effort to be real with ourselves and figure out how we can overcome unhealthy life patterns.

Change cannot come about without hard work.

Our thoughts and words determine our feelings and our feelings determines our actions. When we learn to recognize our patterns of behaviors, then we can work on making the necessary changes. As you reflect on the areas outlined in the Self-Inventory Questionnaire, please be truthful with yourself as you answer the questions and make your comments regarding the topic. Take this platform as a personal journey to change. In these questions, see yourself in your responses. Take this opportunity to improve your life, to take charge of your actions and behaviors by using the power within you to be the person you desire to be. Journal your true thoughts as if you were writing to yourself in a diary. These responses are for your personal benefit; you may see areas in your life where you want to change. Basic dictionary definitions are provided to help you think about the topic area presented.

Each topic area worksheet may be used for mapping exercises (for personal use, in a classroom, or in any setting).

That's Not Who I Am
Self-Inventory Questionnaire

Self

Self is defined as "a person's essential being that distinguishes them from others, especially considered as the object of introspection or reflective action."[1]

"Your self is your sense of who you are, deep down—your identity. When you let someone else know you well, you reveal your true self to them. If the subject of your thoughts is you, you're thinking about your self—or, alternatively, yourself."[2]

How do you define yourself? _____ I am _____, and _____

What qualities do you see in yourself? _____

Do you love yourself?_____

What do you love about yourself?_____

What would you like to change about yourself?_____

and why?_____

Do you like who you are?_____

Have you ever wished you were someone else?_____

_____

_____

_____

_____

---

[1] "Vol 3: Self," The Kindred Voice, accessed January 26, 2023, https://www.thekindredvoice.com/shop/p/vol3self#:~:text=Self%3A%20a%20person's%20essential%20being,of%20introspection%20or%20reflexive%20action.

[2] Vocabulary.com, s.v. "self," accessed February 16, 2023, https://www.vocabulary.com/dictionary/self.

Self-Awareness

"Self-awareness is conscious knowledge of one's own character, feelings, motives, and desires. The ability to take an honest look at your life without attachment to it being right or wrong, good or bad."[3]

Are you aware of your desires?_____

Do you understand your motives?_____

Do you love yourself?_____

Do you demonstrate the ability to be honest with yourself?_____

Can you accept when you are wrong?_____

How would you like to improve your self-awareness skills?_____

_____

_____

_____

_____

_____

_____

_____

_____

---

[3]   Lanre Dahunsi, "Quotes on Self-Awareness," Lanre Dahunsi, posted June 20, 2021, https://lanredahunsi.com/quotes-on-self-awareness/.

Family

A "family is a group of one or more parents and their children living together as a unit."

I would describe my family as_____

My family is known for_____

What have you been told about yourself in your family?_____

I've been told I am_____

I think of myself as_____

What was your childhood like?_____

Happy?_____Not Happy?_____

Other_____

Would you like to be a child again? _____ Yes _____ No.

I am known as_____

I am known for_____in my family_____

_____

_____

_____

_____

_____

Circle of Support

Natural supports can be co-workers, family, or friends

A "Circle of Support is a group of people coming together to help formulate, promote and support the goals of a person. They are people we value in our lives who help us achieve our dreams or lend a hand when we are in need. We all need motivators, people that bring out the best in us. Whenever you around or in the presence of some people or maybe one individual, they make you feel empowered, special, respected, motivated and gifted. This person is your champion because they cheer you on and make you believe you can do anything you want to because they believe in you."

Who are these people in your life?_____

Identify those people by name_____

My circle of support includes_____

I have a circle of support that helps me with_____

My champion in life is_____and_____

I want people to know this about me_____

_____

_____

_____

_____

_____

_____

_____

Friends

A "friend is a person whom one knows and with whom one has a bond of mutual affection, typically exclusive of sexual or family relations."[4]

Do you have many friends?_____

How many close friends do you have?_____

How important are friendships to you?_____

Are you a good, loyal friend?_____

Would you do something wrong for a friend?_____

Have you had a friend betray you or hurt your friendship?_____

How did you resolve the matter?_____

_____

_____

_____

_____

_____

_____

_____

---

[4]   Encyclopedia.com, s.v. "Friend," accessed January 26, 2023, https://www.encyclopedia.com/literature-and-arts/literature-english/english-literature-20th-cent-present/friend#:~:text=friend%20%2F%20frend%2F%20%E2%80%A2%20n.,Friends%20of%20Guilford%20Free%20Library.

Friends at School

Friends at school are important for our social development.

I feel socially awkward at school because_____

I make friends easily because_____

My friends think I am_____My peers say I am _____

I don't think my teachers like me because_____

My teachers say I am_____

I have thoughts of hurting someone else at school because_____

I don't like to talk much because_____

I bully others because_____

I like to fight because_____

I am outgoing and I have a lot of friends because_____

My favorite thing to do is_____

_____

_____

_____

_____

_____

Relationships

A "relationship is the way two or more people connect."

What are your boundaries in friendships/relationships?_____

Where do you draw the line? How far would you go in a relationship?_____

What would make you stop a relationship?_____

What would make you keep going in a relationship?_____

Are you concerned about consequences of wrong actions in a relationship?_____

Have you experienced negative consequences in a relationship?_____

How did you handle it?_____

What's important in a relationship for you?_____

Are you sensitive to the needs and feelings of others in a relationship?_____

_____

_____

_____

_____

_____

_____

_____

Trust

"Trust is a firm belief in the reliability, truth, or strength of someone or something."[5]

Who do you trust?_____

Why is trust so important to you?_____

Have you been betrayed by someone close to you?_____

Have you broken someone's trust?_____

_____

_____

_____

_____

_____

_____

_____

_____

_____

_____

_____

---

[5] "What is Trust?" BrandonCoussensLMFT, accessed January 26, 2023, https://brandoncoussenslmft.com/
what-is-trust/#:~:text=Trust%20is%20a%20firm%20belief,truth%20of%20someone%20or%20something.

Self-Talk

"Self-Talk is the way you talk to yourself or your inner voice. You may not be aware that you are doing it but you certainly are."[6]

"Self-talk is something you do naturally. People are becoming more aware that positive self-talk is a powerful tool for increasing your self-confidence and curbing negative emotions. People who can master positive self-talk are thought to be more confident, motivated and productive."[7]

"This inner voice combines conscious thoughts with inbuilt beliefs and biases to create an internal monologue throughout the day."[8]

How to practice self-talk

Practice daily

1. "Don't fall into negative self-talk traps…
2. Treat yourself like you would a friend…
3. Make self-care a priority…
4. Limit your exposure to negativity…
5. Practice gratitude…
6. Change your vocabulary…
7. Take a timeout…[and]
8. Post positive affirmations."[9]

"There are three kinds of self-talk, positive, negative and instructional."

---

6   "Self-talk," Health Direct, accessed January 26, 2023, https://www.healthdirect.gov.au/self-talk.
7   Susan York Morris, "What Are the Benefits of Self-Talk?" Healthline, last updated December 19, 2016, https://www.healthline.com/health/mental-health/self-talk.
8   "Self-talk."
9   DPS Staff, "10 Ways to Practice Positive Self-Talk," Delaware Psychological Associates, posted April 23, 2021, https://www.delawarepsychologicalservices.com/post/10-ways-to-practice-positive-self-talk.

Positive Self-Talk

"Positive Self Talk is an inner dialogue that makes a person feel good about themselves."

Do you talk to yourself?_____

Do you talk yourself out of negative thoughts?_____

Do you use positive self—talk/thoughts and statements to keep motivated?_____

_____

_____

_____

_____

_____

_____

_____

_____

_____

_____

_____

_____

Negative Self-Talk

"Negative Self-Talk is any negative inner dialogue that could be limiting your ability to believe in yourself and your own abilities to reach your potential. It is any thought that reduces you and your ability to make positive changes in your life or your confidence to do so."[10]

"Negative Self-Talk can come from a place of depression, low-self-confidence, anxiety and can be a part of a more significant mental health concern. However, you may have habits that are causing negative self-talk."

Do you experience negative self-talk?_____

What does your inner dialogue say to you?_____

Can you identify when negative self-talk happens?_____

How are you managing negative self-talk?_____

_____

_____

_____

_____

_____

_____

_____

_____

---

10   Cheryl Gale, "Negative Self Talk—What is it and why does it matter?" Proactive Health + Movement, accessed January 26, 2023, https://www.proactivehm.com.au/negative-self-talk-what-is-it-and-why-does-it-matter/#:~:text=Negative%20self%2Dtalk%20is%20any,your%20ability%20to%20do%20so.

Instructional Self-Talk

"Instructional Self-Talk happens when we need to guide ourselves through a specific task, such as learning a new skill. Motivational self-talk is usually used when we want to psych ourselves up for something challenging. It can help to boost effort or increase confidence."[11]

How have you used instructional self-talk?

Share how you boosted your self-confidence.

Practice self-talking yourself through a challenging situation.

Tell yourself, "I got this."

_____

_____

_____

_____

_____

_____

_____

_____

_____

11   "How to Use Self-Talk to Improve Performance," PsychCentral, accessed January 26, 2023, https://psychcentral.com/blog/how-to-use-self-talk-to-improve-performance#1.

Culture

"Culture can be defined as all the ways of life including arts, beliefs, and institutions of a population that are passed down from generation to generation. Culture has been called 'the way of life for an entire society.' As such it includes codes of manners, dress, language, religion, rituals, art."[12]

What is your culture like?

Are you proud of your culture?

Do you identify with your culture?

Do you choose to identify with the culture of others?

How do you fit into your culture?

What would you like to change?

_____

_____

_____

_____

_____

_____

_____

12 Wayne W. LaMorte, "What is Culture?" Boston University School of Public Health, last modified May 3, 2016, https://sphweb.bumc.bu.edu/otlt/mph-modules/PH/CulturalAwareness/CulturalAwareness2. html#:~:text=Culture%20can%20be%20defined%20as,%2C%20religion%2C%20rituals%2C%20art.

Cultural Competency

Cultural competence is effective "communication with people of other cultures."[13] It has also been defined as the "ability to understand, appreciate and interact with people from cultures or belief systems different from one's own"[14] and the "ability to be diverse and to accept diversity."

Are you culturally competent? Do you accept other cultures?_____

Are you interested in being diverse?_____

Do you respect the views of other cultures?_____

What works for you and your family?_____

_____

_____

_____

_____

_____

_____

_____

_____

_____

_____

---

[13] Wikipedia.com, s.v. "Cultural competence," last updated January 19, 2023, https://en.wikipedia.org/wiki/Cultural_competence.

[14] Tori DeAngelis, "In search of cultural competence," *Monitor on Psychology* 46, no. 3 (March 1, 2015): 64, https://www.apa.org/monitor/2015/03/cultural-competence.

Influences

"Influence is having an effect on the behavior of someone or something."

Are you an influencer for goodwill?_____

Who has been a role model in your life?_____

Who has been a positive influence in your life?_____

What or who has influenced your goals in life?_____

What has been a negative influence in your life?_____

How have you reacted negatively?_____

Are you a people pleaser?_____

What can you do differently?_____

How can you do better?_____

_____

_____

_____

_____

_____

_____

_____

_____

$\mathcal{R}$espect

"Respect means that you accept somebody for who they are; even when they are different from you or you don't agree with them. Respect in relationships build trust, safety, and wellbeing. Respect does not have to come naturally—it is something you learn."[15]

I feel respected when_____

How do you respect others?_____

I respect others when I_____

How do you want to be respected?_____

I want to be respected by_____

How do you see respect displayed today?_____

How can you do better?_____

What will you work on changing?_____

_____

_____

_____

_____

_____

_____

_____

---

[15]   "All About Respect," Kidshelpline, last updated October 17, 2017, https://kidshelpline.com.au/teens/issues/all-about-respect#:~:text=Respect%20means%20that%20you%20accept,it%20is%20something%20you%20learn.

Disrespect

"To disrespect someone is to act in an insulting way toward them. When you disrespect people, you think very little of them. Disrespect is all about not showing respect. Actually, it's about showing the opposite of respect, by acting rude, impolite, and offensive."[16] How do you react when you are disrespected?_____

How do you feel when you are not invited to a party and all your friends are invited?

_____

How do you respond?_____

Do you feel disrespected?_____

Have you disrespected your friends?_____

Your parent?_____

Do you have a habit of disrespecting others?_____

Did you feel remorse?_____

Did you feel a need to apologize?_____

Have you disrespected your teacher?_____

Have you been disrespectful in a relationship?_____

What would you like to change about times when you were disrespectful?_____

Does it matter to you that being disrespectful is not good behavior?_____

Why?_____

---

16 Vocabulary.com, s.v. "disrespect," accessed January 26, 2023, https://www.vocabulary.com/dictionary/disrespect#:
~:text=To%20disrespect%20someone%20is%20to,rude%2C%20impolite%2C%20and%20offensive.

Self-Discipline

"Self-Discipline is the ability to control one's feelings and overcome one's weaknesses; the ability to pursue what one thinks is right despite temptations to abandon it. Self-Discipline is correction or regulation of oneself for the sake of improvement."[17]

How do you control your behavior to do the right thing when all of your friends are enticing or provoking you to do the wrong thing?

_____

How have you demonstrated self-discipline?_____

_____

_____

_____

_____

_____

_____

_____

_____

---

17   Ralph Jabbour, "The Importance of Cultivating Self-Discipline," Entrepreneur, posted November 29, 2017, https://www.entrepreneur.com/en-ae/growth-strategies/the-importance-of-cultivating-self-discipline/305350#:~:text=Self%2Ddiscipline%2C%20by%20definition%2C,achieve%2C%20and%20dreams%20to%20chase.

Stress Management

"Stress is a state of mental or emotional strain or tension resulting from adverse or very demanding circumstances."[18]

Taking deep breaths helps to clear your mind. Research has shown that taking deep breaths sends a message to the brain to calm down. Life challenges may bring on stressful situations at home, at school, with friends, on our jobs, or even when we are just having fun.

There is good stress and bad stress. We have to decide how to manage it.

How do you deal with stress?_____

How do you control your thoughts?_____

How do manage negative situations that bring on stressful behaviors?_____

Who do you talk to?_____

How can you improve the way you manage stress in your life?_____

What do you want to change?_____

_____

_____

_____

_____

_____

_____

---

18   "Managing Stress," Center for Health Advocacy & Wellness, Florida State University, accessed January 23, 2023, https://chaw.fsu.edu/topics/wellness/managing-stress#:~:text=Stress%20is%20the%20state%20of,also%20be%20emotional%20or%20behavioral.

Finances/Money Matters

Finance is the management of money.

Do you have money management problems?_____

Do you reliably pay your debts?_____

Have you had a conflict with someone over money?_____

How did you respond?_____

Have you lost friendship or a relationship due to poor handling of money?_____

How did you fix the situation?_____

Have you sought out help with money management?_____

_____

_____

_____

_____

_____

_____

_____

_____

_____

Responsibilities

"Responsibility is defined as 'the state or fact of having a duty to deal with something or of having control over someone' and 'the state or fact of being accountable or to blame for something.'"[19]

How are you responsible in your behavior or actions?

Have you not met your obligations or responsibilities at

_____ home?

_____ school?

_____ in your community?

_____ in a relationship?

_____ on your job?

What would you like to change to become more responsible?_____

Is being responsible important to you?_____

_____

_____

_____

_____

_____

_____

19 Julie Leoni, "Responsibility, control and power," Julie Leoni, posted February 21, 2015, https://www.julieleoni.com/blog/relationships-and-family/responsibility-control-and-power/#:~:text=Responsibility%20is%20defined%20as%20'the,or%20to%20blame%20for%20something.

Hurt

"Hurt is mental or emotional pain caused by someone."

Have you been hurt?_____

Who hurt you?_____

Do you want to hurt the one who hurt you?_____

What are your thoughts about revenge?_____

How do you move on and work through it?_____

How do you forgive?_____

_____

_____

_____

_____

_____

_____

_____

_____

_____

Being Stuck

"Being Stuck is having a strong desire to do something that will get you out of your current state, but you can't, it's like you are frozen."

Are you stuck?_____

Stuck in a relationship?_____

Stuck in a job?_____

Stuck in past hurts?_____

Stuck in debt?_____

How will you get unstuck?_____

Who can help you get unstuck?_____

When will you do it?_____

_____

_____

_____

_____

_____

_____

_____

_____

Judgement

"Being judgmental is having or displaying an excessively critical point of view. It is easy to be judgmental of others without being aware we are being so."

Do you judge others?_____

Have you been told that you are very critical?_____

Have you hurt someone because you were judgmental?_____

What would you like to do differently?_____

How do you feel when others judge you?_____

Are you critical of others and may not be aware?_____

How do you handle criticism from others?_____

What would you like to change?_____

_____

_____

_____

_____

_____

_____

_____

Power

"Power is possession of control, authority or influence over others."[20]

Do you feel that you have power?_____

How do you handle power in your life?_____

Are you a positive influence with the power you possess?_____

Do you try to control others with the authority you have?_____

Are you using the power you have to change things for the better in your life and in the lives of others around you?

_____

_____

_____

_____

_____

_____

_____

_____

_____

_____

---

[20]   Merriam-Webster.com, s.v. "power," accessed January 26, 2023, https://www.merriam-webster.com/dictionary/power.

Grief

"Grief is deep sorrow, especially that is caused by someone's death; trouble or annoyance. Grief is a normal reaction to a great loss. We can only handle it by taking one day at a time."

How have you handled grief in your life?_____

Were you bitter and angry?_____

Did you take out your anger out on others?_____

How have you helped others through their grief?_____

Did you seek help?_____

_____

_____

_____

_____

_____

_____

_____

_____

_____

Patience

"Patience is the capacity to accept or tolerate delay, trouble, or suffering without getting angry or upset."[21]

Is patience one of your strengths?_____

How have you demonstrated patience?_____

How have you shown impatience?_____

How has being impatient impacted your life?_____

What would you like to change?_____

_____

_____

_____

_____

_____

_____

_____

_____

_____

_____

---

[21]   Parker Klein, "2 Different Types of Patience," Medium, posted January 22, 2022, https://medium.com/twosapp/2-different-types-of-patience-2cd39201ef2b.

Mistakes

"Mistakes *[sic]* an action or judgement that is misguided or wrong; something that is not correct, an inaccuracy. We all make mistakes in life."

What mistakes have you made in your life?_____

How have your mistakes impacted your life?_____

How have you tried to correct the wrongs?_____

What would you like to change?_____

What would you like to do differently?_____

What can you do to not make the same mistake again?_____

_____

_____

_____

_____

_____

_____

_____

_____

_____

_____

Blame

"Blame is to assign responsibility for a fault or wrong." "To blame someone for something is to hold them responsible for something negative that happened. In other words, to blame them is to say or believe that they did it or that it happened because of them."[22]

Who have you blamed for something?_____

Do you take responsibility for your actions or do you blame others?_____

Has someone blamed you falsely?_____

How did you respond?_____

What would you like to change?_____

_____

_____

_____

_____

_____

_____

_____

_____

_____

_____

---

22   Dictionary.com, s.v. "blame," accessed January 26, 2023, https://www.dictionary.com/browse/blame#:~:text=What%20does%20blame%20mean%3F,accused%20of%20having%20committed%20it.

Attitude

"Attitude is a settled way of thinking or feeling about someone or something, typically one that is reflected in a person's behavior…uncooperative behavior, a resentful or antagonistic manner."[23]

Attitude is everything.

What kind of attitude do you have?_____

What have you been told about your attitude by your peers?_____

What have you been told about your attitude by your parents?_____

What have you been told about your attitude at work or school?_____

How can you improve your attitude?_____

How has your attitude prevented you from progressing?_____

_____

_____

_____

_____

_____

_____

_____

_____

23   Encyclopedia.com, s.v. "attitude," accessed January 26, 2023, https://www.encyclopedia.com/ social-sciences-and-law/political-science-and-government/military-affairs-nonnaval/attitude.

Improvement

"Improvement is a thing that makes things better or is better than something else."

_____

We should always want to improve, advance, and gain more in our lives.

What areas of your life would you like to improve in?_____

How much thought have you given to actually improving in areas needed?_____

What will it take to motivate you to move forward to improve?_____

What has been an obstacle to your improvement?_____

_____

_____

_____

_____

_____

_____

_____

_____

_____

_____

Deception

"Deception is the act of causing someone to accept as true or valid what is false or invalid. The act of deceiving."[24]

How have you been deceived?_____

How did you respond?_____

Have you deceived others?_____

How did you respond?_____

What would you like to change?_____

_____

_____

_____

_____

_____

_____

_____

_____

_____

_____

---

24   Merriam-Webster.com, s.v. "deception," accessed January 26, 2023, https://www.merriam-webster.com/
dictionary/deception.

Insecure/Insecurity

"Insecurity is uncertainty or anxiety about oneself; lack of confidence."

How have you felt insecure?_____

What makes you feel insecure or uncertain?_____

Who has made you feel insecure?_____

Has this feeling of insecurity caused you to have a lack of self-confidence?_____

What needs to change?_____

_____

_____

_____

_____

_____

_____

_____

_____

_____

_____

_____

_____

Anxiety/Anxious

"Anxiety is persistent worry and fear about everyday situations."

Do you worry a lot about everyday situations?_____

What do you worry about?_____

Who can you talk to about your worries?_____

Where can you go for help?_____

Who can you depend on?_____

How do you get your worrying under control?_____

Are you hiding anything that bothers you?_____

Are you worrying about it?_____

How does it make you feel?_____

_____

_____

_____

_____

_____

_____

_____

Arrogance

Arrogance is "to exaggerate one's own worth or importance often by an overbearing manner."[25] "Having or showing an exaggerated opinion of one's own importance, merit, ability, conceited, overbearingly proud."

How have you demonstrated arrogance?_____

Have you been told that you are arrogant?_____

What would you like to change?_____

_____

_____

_____

_____

_____

_____

_____

_____

_____

_____

_____

[25] Merriam-Webster.com, s.v. "arrogant," accessed January 26, 2023, https://www.merriam-webster.com/dictionary/arrogant.

Guilt

"Guilt is feeling responsible or regretful for a perceived offense."

How does guilt make you feel?_____

Do you feel guilty about anything?_____

Does it bother you_____that you_____?

Do you want to make it right?_____

What do you want to change about the feeling of guilt you are experiencing?_____

How do you fix it?_____

_____

_____

_____

_____

_____

_____

_____

_____

_____

_____

Honesty

"Honesty is being truthful, telling the truth, It is often said, 'Honesty is the best policy.' Honesty is the best policy means telling the truth is better than lying even when it is hard to do."

Are you one who tells the truth?_____

Are you a liar?_____

Does lying bother you? Yes or no and why?_____

_____

_____

_____

_____

_____

_____

_____

_____

_____

_____

Teasing

To tease is "to make fun of, to disturb or annoy by persistent irritating or provoking especially in a mischievous way."[26]

Do you tease other people, put them down, and laugh at their shortcomings?

_____

How does that make you feel?_____

How would you feel if someone teased you?_____

What would you do if someone teased someone you cared about?_____

Do you feel remorse?_____

Do you feel lonely sometimes, not at all, or all the time?

_____

_____

_____

_____

_____

_____

_____

_____

_____

---

26 Merriam-Webster.com, s.v. "tease," accessed January 23, 2023, https://www.merriam-webster.com/dictionary/tease.

Hatred

"Hatred is intense dislike or ill will toward someone or something."

What do you hate?_____

Who do you hate?_____

How do you deal with hate and hateful thoughts?_____

_____

_____

_____

_____

_____

_____

_____

_____

_____

_____

_____

_____

Retaliation

"Retaliation is to get revenge, to repay."

How do you retaliate?_____

Do you seek revenge?_____

Do you let things go when you have been offended?_____

_____

_____

_____

_____

_____

_____

_____

_____

_____

_____

_____

_____

_____

Expectation

An expectation is "a strong belief that something will happen or be the case in the future."[27]

What do you expect from others?_____

What do you expect?_____

Do you feel whole or complete? If not, why not?_____

Are you a truthful person? Will you tell the truth? Will you tell the whole truth or part of the truth?

_____

Will you say things are okay when they are not? Even when it's obvious things are not okay?

_____

_____

_____

_____

_____

_____

_____

_____

---

[27] Encyclopedia.com, s.v. "expectation," accessed January 23, 2023, https://www.encyclopedia.com/science-and-technology/computers-and-electrical-engineering/computers-and-computing/expectation.

Hopes

"Hopes are what you would desire or want to happen."

I hope that_____

My hope is for my family to_____and_____for me.

Sometimes I feel like there is_____hope for_____and I_____

I sure hope_____happens in my life

_____

_____

_____

_____

_____

_____

_____

_____

_____

_____

_____

Capacities

Capacities are what you are good at, your abilities.

What are your capacities?_____

Who has helped you to see your capacities?_____

How have you developed your capacities?_____

_____

_____

_____

_____

_____

_____

_____

_____

_____

_____

_____

_____

_____

Trouble

To trouble is "to agitate mentally or spiritually; worry [or] disturb."[28] Trouble is easy to get into and hard to get out of.

What troubles you?_____

Who troubles you?_____

When do you get into trouble?_____

Who influences you to get into trouble?_____

When you are in trouble, who do you call?_____

Where do you get your answers to difficult problems?_____

How do you handle distress?_____

_____

_____

_____

_____

_____

_____

_____

---

28   Merriam-Webster.com, s.v. "trouble," accessed January 27, 2023, https://www.merriam-webster.com/dictionary/trouble.

$\mathcal{D}$isappointment

Disappointment is "sadness or displeasure by the nonfulfillment of one's hopes or expectations."[29]

_____disappointed me and I feel_____

I feel bad because I think I disappointed_____

I was disappointed in myself when_____

If I could change_____it would be_____

_____

_____

_____

_____

_____

_____

_____

_____

_____

_____

_____

_____

_____

---

[29] Encyclopedia.com, s.v. "disappointment," accessed January 27, 2023, https://www.encyclopedia.com/humanities/dictionaries-thesauruses-pictures-and-press-releases/disappointment.

Authority

Authority is having power or control in situations.

What authority do you have?_____

How do you respond when someone tells you what to do?_____

Do you respect authority?_____

Do you understand the importance of respecting authority?_____

Are you disrespectful to the authority of

_____ parents?

_____ the elderly?

_____ teachers?

_____ coaches?

_____ your spouse?

_____ children?

_____ pastors?

_____ friends?

_____ employers?

_____ neighbors?

_____ coworkers?

_____ law enforcement?

_____ others?

Escaping

To "escape is to break free from confinement or control."

Where do you escape to?_____

My get away place is_____

My favorite thing to do that makes me feel great is_____

I will escape when_____happens.

_____

_____

_____

_____

_____

_____

_____

_____

_____

_____

_____

_____

_____

Thoughts

Thoughts are what you think about.

My thoughts are important because_____

What do you think about?_____

Are your thoughts positive?_____

How can you improve upon your positive thinking?_____

Are your thoughts negative?_____

How can you change your negative thought patterns?_____

How do you view or think about yourself?_____

How do you view or think about others?_____

Do you harbor ill thoughts about other cultures, races, or ethnicities?_____

If so, why?_____

How can you change your negative view of others?_____

Do you care about the thoughts of others?_____

How do you have a good balance between your thoughts and what others think of you?

_____

What would you like to change about yourself?_____

_____

_____

Belief

Belief is trust, faith, or confidence in something.

I believe_____

_____believes in me.

I believe in_____

I wish_____believed in me because_____

I need_____to believe in me because_____

_____

_____

_____

_____

_____

_____

_____

_____

_____

_____

_____

Giving/Lending a Helping Hand

Giving is providing love or other emotional support.

I have a desire to give to others when I_____and when I_____

I give of myself by_____and_____

I like when_____gives me_____and_____

I feel_____when I give_____

_____

_____

_____

_____

_____

_____

_____

_____

_____

_____

_____

Care

Caring is showing kindness to others.

I care a lot about_____because of_____and_____

I don't care about_____because_____

_____does not care about me so I don't care about_____

I don't care what_____thinks about me_____

_____shows kindness to me and I_____

_____

_____

_____

_____

_____

_____

_____

_____

_____

_____

_____

Change

To "change is to replace something with something else."

I would like to change_____, and_____in my life,

because_____

I don't like it when I_____because_____always happens.

I try to do better but_____gets in my way each time I_____

I keep making the same mistake because of_____and_____

I can't control my_____because_____

I need_____to help me with_____and_____

I need to change my bad habit of_____because_____

If I don't change my_____it's going to hinder me greatly when I try to_____

I want to change because I don't like it when_____

I want to change because I have hurt others when I_____

I want to change and become a better person because_____and_____

I do not want to be known as_____or_____

I am willing to work on_____.to change my_____behavior.

I want to change for_____and_____

I know I was wrong when I_____and I want to_____

Anger

"Anger is a strong feeling of hostility."

_____makes me angry and_____helps me to_____

My anger looks like_____and_____

When I am angry, I do wrong things such as_____and_____t

I have trouble controlling my anger, so I_____

and_____to help me manage my anger.

Anger is a problem for me, so I_____and_____

What hinders you?_____Does your anger hinder you?_____

If yes, why?_____

_____

Recall an incident when you were very angry. How did you handle it? Were you satisfied with your response? What could you have done differently?

_____

_____

_____

_____

_____

_____

Bullying

"Bullying is seeking to harm, intimidate or coerce someone perceived as vulnerable."

Bullying is_____and it makes me feel_____for_____and_____

How did you feel? I felt_____and_____when I was bullied.

When I was bullied, I_____and_____and told_____

What did you want to do that you knew you should not do?_____

When I was bullied, I wanted to_____and_____but I knew that I should not do that.

Did you do_____and_____because you were bullied?

What happened when you made the wrong decision while bullying?_____

What happened when you made the wrong decision while being bullied?_____

How did it work out?_____

How did you feel about yourself after you decided to bully?_____

There are consequences for bullying, and I don't want to be responsible for_____

_____and_____

Do you bully others?_____

_____

_____

_____

_____

Integrity

"Integrity is being honest and having strong moral principles; being upright."

I try to be honest about_____and_____

It bothers me when I don't_____and_____

I respect others that demonstrate that they are_____and_____

_____

_____

_____

_____

_____

_____

_____

_____

_____

_____

_____

_____

Rejection

"Rejection is the dismissal or the refusal of an idea or someone."

_____made me feel rejected.

Rejection makes me want to_____to someone.

I want to get rid of this feeling of rejection because it causes me to_____

and_____

My friends rejected me so I_____and_____them.

My parents rejected me and I decided to_____and_____

I have never felt more rejected than when I_____and_____

I felt rejected when I was not invited to_____

I felt rejected when I was not selected to participate in_____

I felt rejected when I was not picked for_____

I felt rejected by my coworkers so I_____and_____and told my coworkers

that_____was not necessary.

How did you respond?_____What would you like to change?_____

_____

_____

_____

_____

Remorse

"Remorse is deep regret or guilt for a wrong committed."

I felt remorse when I_____and I wanted to_____but_____

I regret_____and_____.

I felt guilty when I_____and_____to_____

I wish I had not_____to_____

_____

_____

_____

_____

_____

_____

_____

_____

_____

_____

_____

_____

Decision Making

"Decision Making is making a course of action among several possible alternatives."

I made the wrong decision about_____and I had to_____

I have often decided to_____but I did_____Instead

I want to make better, wiser decisions because_____

I realize there are consequences regarding the decisions I made so I want to_____and

_____the next time.

_____

_____

_____

_____

_____

_____

_____

_____

_____

_____

_____

Betrayal

"Betrayal is when someone you trust breaks that trust by doing something that hurts you."

Have you been betrayed by somcone you trust?_____

Have you betrayed someone?_____

How did feel about it?_____

Were you accused wrongly?_____Was there a misunderstanding?

What does the pain of betrayal feel like?_____

What would like to change?_____

_____

_____

_____

_____

_____

_____

_____

_____

_____

_____

_____

Denial

"Denial is refusing to admit the truth or reality of something unpleasant."

How have you been in denial?_____

What have you been in denial about?_____

How can you get to the point of acceptance of the truth?_____

What would you like to change?_____

_____

_____

_____

_____

_____

_____

_____

_____

_____

_____

_____

_____

Road Rage

Road rage is aggressive or angry behavior exhibited by motorist.

How do you manage yourself in hectic traffic?_____

When in hectic traffic, I_____and_____

When someone cuts over in my lane, I_____but I know I should_____

If someone yells verbal insults at me, or blows the horn at me, I_____and_____

_____

_____

_____

_____

_____

_____

_____

_____

_____

_____

_____

Mass Shootings

A "mass shooting is an incident involving the shooting with one or more firearms of a number of people; where at least four people are hit by gunfire."

I think mass shootings are_____because of_____and_____

Mass shootings are senseless killings because_____

I felt_____when I heard of the mass shootings across the country

because_____

_____

_____

_____

_____

_____

_____

_____

_____

_____

_____

Police Brutality

"Police Brutality is the excessive and unwarranted use of force by law enforcement against an individual or a group. It is an extreme form of police misconduct."[30]

I think police brutality is_____and_____

I have witnessed police brutality when_____

If I get into a situation with the police, I will_____and_____to avoid conflict.

_____

_____

_____

_____

_____

_____

_____

_____

_____

_____

_____

—————
[30] Wikipedia.com, s.v. "Police brutality," accessed January 27, 2023, https://en.wikipedia.org/wiki/Police_brutality.

Racial Profiling

"Racial profiling or ethnic profiling is the act of suspecting, targeting or discriminating against a person on the basis of their ethnicity, religion or nationality, rather than on individual suspicion or available evidence."[31]

Have you experienced racial profiling?_____

How would you handle yourself if you were racially profiled?_____

_____

_____

_____

_____

_____

_____

_____

_____

_____

_____

_____

[31] Wikipedia.com, s.v. "Racial profiling," accessed January 27, 2023, https://en.wikipedia.org/wiki/Racial_profiling.

Abortion

"The deliberate termination of a human pregnancy."

How do you feel about abortion rights or personal freedoms?_____

Who can you talk to about abortion or abortion rights?_____

Are you angry about abortion rights in this country?_____

_____

_____

_____

_____

_____

_____

_____

_____

_____

_____

_____

_____

Forgiveness

"Psychologists generally define forgiveness as a conscious, deliberate decision to release feelings of resentment or vengeance toward a person or group, who has harmed you, regardless of whether they actually deserve your forgiveness."[32]

Is it easy to forgive?_____

Who do you need to forgive?_____

Who do you want to forgive you?_____

I find it hard to forgive_____because of_____

I need help to forgive_____

because of_____

_____

_____

_____

_____

_____

_____

_____

_____

---

32 "What is forgiveness?" Greater Good Magazine, accessed February 16, 2023, https://greatergood.berkeley.edu/topic/forgiveness/definition#:~:text=I%20Cultivate%20It%3F-,What%20Is%20Forgiveness%3F,they%20actually%20deserve%20your%20forgiveness.

Being Appreciated

Appreciation is recognition and enjoyment of the good qualities of someone or something.

Who would miss you if you were not here?_____

Who appreciates you?_____

How have you been shown appreciation?_____

_____

_____

_____

_____

_____

_____

_____

_____

_____

_____

_____

_____

Self-Esteem

"Self Esteem is confidence in one's own worth or abilities, self–respect. Self-esteem encompasses beliefs about oneself as well as emotional states, such as triumph, despair, pride, and shame."[33]

Who builds you up?_____

Who puts a smile on your face?_____

Who do you want to become?_____

Do you think you cannot become_____because_____?.

You do know that you can become_____and_____

Who told you you could never become_____?

What do you do when obstacles confront you?_____

How do you overcome failure?_____

How do you deal with defeat?_____

What do you constantly struggle with?_____

Who do you talk to?_____

What do you bottle up inside that you feel you can't tell anyone?_____

What are your fears?_____Why are you afraid?_____

What makes you happy?_____

Who tells you that you can do anything you want to because you *can* do it?_____

What do you want to change about you and/or your life?_____

---

[33] Wikipedia.com, s.v. "Self-esteem," accessed January 27, 2023, https://en.wikipedia.org/wiki/Self-esteem.

Things I Am Sorry for Doing

I Know Better than That

I knew better when I_____and_____

Why did I do_____?

I apologized for_____

I knew better, but I did_____anyway.

I am sorry for_____

I was not raised by my parents to_____and_____

I made it right when I_____to_____

_____

_____

_____

_____

_____

_____

_____

_____

Self-Control

"Self-control...is the ability to regulate one's emotions, thoughts, and behavior in the face of temptations and impulses."[34]

I could not control myself when I_____and_____

I want to reach my goals, so I have to stop_____and_____

My lack of self-control has caused me to not be able to_____, and_____

I need to learn to self-regulate because_____

Things I Would like to See Different about Myself

What would you like to see different about yourself?_____

If you could turn back the hands of time, what would you change or do differently?

_____It's not too late.

What are you hiding?_____

What are you ashamed of?_____

What are you embarrassed about?_____

What embarrasses you?_____

Have you ever been humiliated?_____Humiliated publicly?_____

How did you handle the situation?_____

_____

---

34   Wikipedia.com, s.v. "Self-control," accessed January 27, 2023, https://en.wikipedia.org/wiki/Self-control#:~:
      text=Self%2Dcontrol%2C%20an%20aspect%20of,order%20to%20achieve%20specific%20goals.

Happiness

"Happiness is an emotional state characterized by feelings of joy, satisfaction, contentment and fulfillment."[35]

Who brings you joy?_____

Who do you want to make proud?_____

What brings you satisfaction?_____

Who do want to impress?_____

What do you want to fulfill in your life?_____and_____

_____

_____

_____

_____

_____

_____

_____

_____

_____

_____

"What is Happiness?" Verywellmind, last updated November 7, 2022, https://www.verywellmind.com/what-is-happiness-4869755.

Fears

"Fear is a hindrance to growth, development and change."

Who are you afraid of?_____

Who terrifies you?_____

What makes you feel so afraid that you are frozen in your tracks?_____

Who makes you feel safe and secure?_____

_____

_____

_____

_____

_____

_____

_____

_____

_____

_____

_____

_____

Desire

"Desire is a strong feeling of wanting to have something or wishing for something to happen."

What are your desires?_____

What are your hopes for now and for the future?_____

What do you want that you do not have?_____

What would you do to get your desires met?_____

Would you do anything to get it?_____

_____

_____

_____

_____

_____

_____

_____

_____

_____

_____

_____

Abuse

"Abuse is to treat a person or animal with cruelty or violence."

"Thoughts of abuse lingers long into our adulthood and life time and can hinder positive change, if we allow it to."

Have you been abused physically?_____

Have you been abused emotionally?_____

Have you been abused sexually?_____

Have you received professional help regarding the abuse?_____

Do you want to talk about it with someone, such as a professional counselor or a pastor?

_____

_____

_____

_____

_____

_____

_____

_____

_____

Deficits

"Deficits are temporary setbacks that can be changed to strengths if we want them to be changed."

What are your deficits?_____

Do you focus on your deficits?_____ Yes_____ No_____

What are you willing to change in your life?_____

What can you do to improve your deficits_____? _____and_____

Who do you need to help you?_____and_____

What do you need to help you?_____

_____

_____

_____

_____

_____

_____

_____

_____

_____

Triggers

"Trigger—cause (an event or situation) to happen or exist. Recognizing your triggers are essential to learning how to manage your triggers."

What is a trigger for you?_____

How do manage your triggers?_____

What would you like to change?_____

_____

_____

_____

_____

_____

_____

_____

_____

_____

_____

_____

Strength

"Strength is power to resist attacks, endurance, toughness, being strong."

What are your strengths?

My strengths are_____and_____and_____

I am not sure what I am strong in but I want to find out_____

I have been told that I am really strong at_____and_____

I feel_____is a strength but I am not sure because_____

I need to think about what my strengths are because_____

I am confident that my strengths are_____and_____

_____

_____

_____

_____

_____

_____

_____

_____

_____

Family Expectations

"Expectation is expecting or anticipation of what would happen."

Everyone in my family does_____well.

I don't want to do_____

I am expected to_____

I have my own expectations for my future and my expectations are_____

and_____

I am not sure what I expect of myself in the future_____

because_____

My role model is_____

Who do you desire to be like?_____I want to be_____but_____

Who do you not want to be like?_____

_____is my hero.

_____

_____

_____

_____

_____

Personality

"Personality is an individual's distinctive character, patterns of thinking, feeling and behaving."

What is your personality like?_____

Are you generous?_____

Protective of friends?_____

Caring?_____

A perfectionist?_____

Loyal?_____

A loner?_____

Outgoing?_____

What would you like to change?_____

_____

_____

_____

_____

_____

_____

_____

Love

Love is "an intense feeling of deep affection."[36]

Do you feel loved?_____

Who do you love?_____

Who loves you?_____

How do you express your love?_____

How do you want to be loved by others?_____

Who knows you?_____

Do you love yourself? _____ Yes _____ No

What's important to you that you want others to know about? _____

Who do you depend on?_____

Who depends on you?_____

What makes you feel needed, wanted, and/or accepted?_____

_____

_____

_____

_____

36   Sarah Arscott, "What is Love?" Medium, posted July 13, 2020, https://medium.com/fearless-she-wrote/what-is-love-7695a6f9b23f.

Assertive

Being assertive "is having or showing a confident and forceful personality. Being assertive shows that you respect yourself because you are willing to stand up for your interests and express your thoughts and feelings."

Are you assertive in your interactions with others?_____

Did you have to learn to be assertive?_____

Who were you assertive with?_____

How has being assertive benefited you?_____

What would you like to change?_____

_____

_____

_____

_____

_____

_____

_____

_____

_____

Failures

"Failures are pathways, stepping stones to overcoming defeats."

How have you failed in your life?_____

Who failed you?_____

Who have you failed?_____

How do you want to change that failure?_____

_____

_____

_____

_____

_____

_____

_____

_____

_____

_____

_____

_____

_____

$Coerced$

"Being coerced into negative actions is doing something against your better judgment but you did it anyway."

I was coerced into doing_____

I did_____I did not like_____

I don't ever want to do_____again.

I learned how to_____from_____

_____

_____

_____

_____

_____

_____

_____

_____

_____

_____

_____

Peer Pressure

"Peer Pressure is when you are influenced by other people (your peers) to act in a certain way. If you're with friends who are doing something that you typically would not do and they convince you to do what they are doing, that is an example of peer pressure."[37]

Do you want to be liked by your peers?_____

Will you do the wrong thing to fit in?_____

Do you to try what others are doing even when you know it's the wrong thing to do?

_____

How do you handle peer pressure?_____

Who can you talk to about it?_____

_____

_____

_____

_____

_____

_____

_____

_____

---

[37] "What is Peer Pressure?" Study.com, accessed January 27, 2023, https://study.com/academy/lesson/what-is-peer-pressure-definition-lesson-quiz.html.

Who Am I?

Who do you say you are?_____

Who do others say you are?_____

What do other people/peers say about you?_____

I did_____because I want to be accepted, included by_____

I felt_____afterward.

How did you become who you are today?_____

Do you have a nickname? For example,

Killer, T-Murder, Fats, Slim, Shorty, Scarface and so on. _____ Yes _____No

Do you identify with that name? How do you identify with that name?_____

Has someone tried to label you? Have you been labeled?_____

Who were your negative influences?_____

Have you ever been called dumb or stupid? _____ Yes _____ No

Did you believe it? _____Yes _____No

How did it make you feel?_____

_____lies deep inside of you_____

What lies deep inside that you desire to come alive?_____

Who told you that you couldn't?_____

_____

Identification

"Identity is the distinguishing character or personality of an individual."[38]

How do you want to be identified?_____

I am_____

Who told you that you could be anyone you desired to be?_____

I do not want to be identified as_____

I now know who I am because of_____

_____

_____

_____

_____

_____

_____

_____

_____

_____

_____

---

[38] Merriam-Webster.com, s.v. "identity," accessed January 27, 2023, https://www.merriam-webster.com/dictionary/identity.

Workplace

"A place where people work and spend the majority of their day."

I enjoy my job_____because_____

I am good at_____and_____

My coworkers say I am a team player because I_____and

_____

When I have a problem on my job, I report to_____

to avoid_____and_____

I demonstrate good interpersonal skills on my job by demonstrating_____

and_____

My boss describes me as_____

_____

_____

_____

_____

_____

_____

_____

Punctuality

Punctuality is being on time.

Are you a punctual person?_____

How has not being punctual affected your life?_____

Do you think that others have time to wait on you?_____

Do you see the importance of being punctual?_____

Do you value other people's time?_____

Have you ever felt bad because you were late?_____

How did this situation affect you?_____

How have you wanted to change?_____

_____

_____

_____

_____

_____

_____

_____

_____

The Value of Life

What you value are the things that you believe are important in the way you live and work.

Is your life turning out the way you want it to?_____

Do you value life?_____

Do you value the lives of others?_____

Are you capable of killing someone?_____

If so, how do you think you would feel afterward?_____

Do you know someone who killed someone in self-defense?_____

Do you know someone who killed someone because of anger or lack of self control?

_____

Do you want to share what happened?_____

Do you think the person had regrets?_____

Do you believe in an eye for an eye and tooth for a tooth philosophy?_____

Share your thoughts on this philosophy_____

_____

_____

_____

_____

Inappropriate Sexual Behavior

"Inappropriate sexual behavior or sexually aggressive behavior, is a term which encompasses a variety of behaviors, including Obscene gesturing, touching or hugging another person, exposing body parts or disrobing, and masturbating in public."[39]

What are your thoughts on inappropriate sexual behavior?

_____

_____

What is disturbing about this type of behavior?

_____

_____

_____

_____

_____

_____

_____

_____

[39]   S.W. Philo, M.F. Richie, and M.J. Kaas, "Inappropriate Sexual Behavior," *Journal of Gerontological Nursing* 22, no. 1 (November 1996): 17–22, https://doi.org/10.3928/0098-9134-19961101-07.

Gun Violence

"Gun-related violence is violence committed with the use of a firearm."[40]

"Gun violence is a leading cause of premature death in the U.S."[41]

Firearms recently became the number one cause of death for children and teens in the U. S surpassing motor vehicles and those caused by other injuries"

"Firearms recently became the number one cause of death for children in the United States, surpassing motor vehicle deaths and those caused by other injuries."[42]

Do you own a gun?_____

Have you had gun safety classes?_____

Are your guns in a locked case?_____

What do you plan to use your gun for?_____

What are your thoughts on gun violence in this country?_____

What would you like to change?_____

What would you like to see changed in this country?_____

_____

_____

---

40 Wikipedia.com, s.v. "Gun violence," last updated February 16, 2023, https://en.wikipedia.org/wiki/Gun_violence.

41 "Gun Violence," American Public Health Association, accessed February 16, 2023, https://www.apha.org/topics-and-issues/gun-violence.

42 Matt McGough, Krutika Amin, Nirmita Panchal, and Cynthia Cox, "Child and Teen Firearm Mortality in the U.S. and Peer Countries," KFF, posted July 8, 2022, https://www.kff.org/global-health-policy/issue-brief/child-and-teen-firearm-mortality-in-the-u-s-and-peer-countries/.

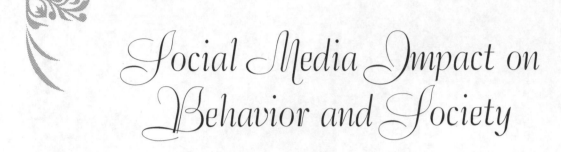

Social Media Impact on Behavior and Society

"Social Media research shows an increasing dependence on social media is resulting in shorter attention spans, poorer memories and reduced reflexes and motor skills. Social Media has created new styles of communication which has made a huge impact on everyday living. Social Media has made a profound impact on human behavior and society. People get rude and express maybe what they normally would not express face to face.

"Social Media can cause mental illness, problems with self-esteem and bullying This can cause problems like arguments and controversy. Disagreements in comment sections cause people to react negatively. Many unhappy people unload their frustrations, people vent their problems and demonstrate their outrage on social media by airing their anger to the world and releasing their build up steam."

How are you impacted by social media?_____

How are you influenced by social media posts?_____

Do you find yourself changing your behavior, attitude, and beliefs since you have experienced social media interactions?

How have you changed?_____

How have you been impacted in a good way?_____

What are the pros?_____

How have you been impacted in a negative way?_____

What are the cons?_____

Why is communicating on social media so important to you?_____

Share your thoughts_____

Would you like to see exceptions to social media mandates?_____

Share your thoughts

How have you become a better person because of social media?_____

Describe a recent situation on social media that was a central issue of conflict and that impacted you.

Share your thoughts.

What was the outcome? How did you handle the situation?

_____

_____

_____

_____

_____

_____

_____

_____

_____

_____

_____

_____

Cyberbullying

"Cyberbullying or cyberharassment is a form of bullying or harassment using electronic means. Cyberbullying and cyberharassment are also known as online bullying."[43]

Have you experienced cyberbullying?_____

Share your thoughts_____

Has cyberbullying impacted your life?_____How?_____

Do you know someone who experienced cyberbullying?_____

How was it handled?_____

What would you like to see changed online with digital technology?_____

_____

_____

_____

_____

_____

_____

_____

_____

---

43 Wikipedia.com, s.v. "Cyberbullying," last updated January 7, 2023, https://en.wikipedia.org/wiki/Cyberbullying.

Family Dynamics

"Family dynamics are the patterns of interactions between family members. These includes roles, hierarchies, and communication between family members."[44] "Because family members rely on each other for emotional, physical, and economic support, they are one of the primary sources of relationship security or stress."[45]

"Family dynamics are how members of a family interact with each other in relation to their individual goals and preferences."[46]

Do you have a favorite sibling?_____

What role do you play in your family?_____

Who do you rely on in your family for support?_____

Who do you communicate well with in your family?_____

Who causes you stress in your family?_____

Who makes you feel secure in your family?_____

Do you have positive examples to follow?_____

What does the hierarchy look like in your family?_____

How have you and your family worked together as a team?_____

_____

_____

---

44 Waters, "Family Dynamics."
45 Bahareh Jabbari and Audra S. Rouster, "Family Dynamics," *StatPearls* [Internet], Treasure Island, FL: StatPearls Publishing, 2022.
46 Waters, "Family Dynamics."

The Influences of Environment

"Contributory factors include material deprivation, poor parental health, low parental education, family stress, exposure to intimate partner violence, neighborhood deprivation, and poor school environment."[47]

What does your home environment look like?_____

Were you deprived of necessities like food, housing, or education?

_____

Were you exposed to any type of family violence? _____

Are your parents in good health? If not in good health, how has their poor health impacted you?

Are your parents educated?_____

Did they finish high school?_____

College?_____

Post College?_____

How does their education or lack of education influenced your life?_____

What would you like to change or see different?_____

_____

_____

_____

47 "Environmental factors that contribute to child vulnerability," OECDLibrary, accessed January 27, 2023, https://www.oecd-ilibrary.org/sites/6a006a25-en/index.html?itemId=/content/component/6a006a25-en.

Substance Abuse

"Substance abuse is over indulgence in or dependence on an addictive substance especially alcohol or drugs."[48] Excessive substance abuse can cause an individual physical or emotional problems and/or impair the individual's social functioning.

Second sentence source is from Oxford Languages when googled the definition of substance abuse.

Have you abused alcohol? _____

Do you feel you are an alcoholic? _____

What kind of help do you need? _____

What triggers your drinking? _____

What would you like to change? _____

Have you abused drugs? _____

Do you feel you are addicted to drugs? _____

What kind of help do you need? _____

What triggers your need for drugs? _____

What would you like to change? _____

Are you willing to get help? _____

Do you have an addiction to over-the-counter drugs such as pain medication?_____

What would you like to change? _____

---

48   "Substance Abuse Among College Students," Affordable Colleges, accessed January 27, 2023, https://www. affordablecollegesonline.org/college-resource-center/substance-abuse-in-college/.

Vaping

"Vaping is an action or practice of inhaling and exhaling vapor containing nicotine and flavoring produced by device designed for this purpose. There's a concern that young people may take up vaping as a less harmful alternative to smoking."

_____

Have you ever used an electronic cigarette? _____

Do you feel you are addicted to vaping? _____

How have you been influenced by your peers to use an electronic cigarette?

_____

_____

_____

_____

_____

_____

_____

_____

_____

_____

Overeating/Overindulging

Symptoms of Overeating

Eating a large amount of food in a specific amount of time, such as over a two-hour period.

_____

Feeling your eating behavior is out of control._____

Eating even when you are full and not hungry._____

Can you identify with any of these symptoms?_____

What triggers your overeating?_____

How does overeating affect your weight, social interactions, and self-esteem?_____

What would you like to change?_____

What would you like to do differently?_____

_____

_____

_____

_____

_____

_____

_____

Exploitation

"Exploitation is the act of selfishly taking advantage of someone or a group of people in order to profit from them or otherwise benefit oneself."[49]

Have you intentionally taken advantage of someone? _____

How did you feel? _____

Has anyone ever stolen from you and misled you? _____

What would you like to change? _____

Has someone taken advantage of you? _____

How did you feel? _____

What would you like to change? _____

_____

_____

_____

_____

_____

_____

49   Dictionary.com, s.v. "exploitation," accessed January 27, 2023, https://www.dictionary.com/browse/exploitation#:~:text=Exploitation%20is%20the%20act%20of,exploitative%2C%20as%20in%20exploitative%20practices.

Neglect of Hopes and Dreams

You neglect your hopes and dreams when your hopes and dreams seem impossible to accomplish. You procrastinate, become discouraged, and get stuck.

What have you not fulfilled in your life? _____

What dreams have been deferred? Why? _____

What are you going to do about it? _____

What are you willing to change to make it happen? _____

_____

_____

_____

_____

_____

_____

_____

_____

_____

_____

_____

Beaten Down

"Being beat[en] down is when someone will not let you up for air. They drag you down, they decrease your self-esteem and make you feel worthless."

Have you experienced being beaten down by someone? _____

How did you feel? _____

How did you respond? _____

Were you accused falsely? _____

Did it make you angry? _____

Did it make you want to fight? _____

Who do you go to for help? _____

How do you get unstuck? _____

_____

_____

_____

_____

_____

_____

_____

Socially Valued Roles

What positive roles do you see yourself in?_____

What negative roles?_____

Give examples of positive roles_____

Give examples of negative roles_____

Do you see yourself as valued?

See examples below. You may add roles not listed.

Circle the role you identify with below.

Student   Mother   Father

Friend   Lawyer   Doctor

Employer

                        Artist

                                              Poet

Parent   Son

_____

_____

_____

_____

_____

Socially Valued Roles
(continued)

Daughter   Teacher   Celebrity

Musician   Grandparent

Cook   Dancer

          Author

Godmother

                    Godfather   Entrepreneur

          Coach

                                        Elected Official

Principal

                          Nurse

Dentist

                                        Employee

Other   Athlete

Goals

A goal is an "object of a person's ambition or effort; an aim or desired result."[50]

What are your short-term goals (goals that you want to reach in the next week, month, six months, year, or other time frame)?

1.

2.

3.

What are your long-term goals (goals that you want to reach in the next five, ten, or fifteen years, or other time frame)?

1.

2.

3.

Have you thought about your future goals, such as goals for your life overall? If so, what are they?

1.

2.

3.

---

50   Brianna Wallace, "The object of a person's ambition or effort; an aim or desired result. Goals," Alexander Muss High School in Israel, posted June 26, 2019, https://www.amhsi.org/amhsi-blog/amhsi-blog/2019/06/26/the-object-of-a-person's-ambition-or-effort-an-aim-or-desired-result.-goals.

Dreams

A dream is "a series of thoughts, images, and sensations occurring in a person's mind. A cherished aspiration, ambition or idea."

What are your dreams?_____

What is on your mind twenty-four-seven that you want to accomplish?_____

What do you want to break through?_____

What do you want to complete?_____

What do you want in order to feel satisfied?_____

What do you want to get out of the box?_____

What do you want in order to feel proud of yourself?_____

_____

_____

_____

_____

_____

_____

_____

_____

Education

"Education is being educated, learning, gaining knowledge in school or other settings."

Do you value education?_____

Did your parents or siblings finish their education journeys?_____

What goals do you want to work on to finish your education?_____

_____

School requires being focused. Do you lack focus?

_____

Are you focused on finishing school?_____

What barriers are preventing you from accomplishing your education goals?_____

What are your plans after you have completed your education?_____

High school_____

College_____

Post College_____

_____

_____

_____

_____

_____

Ancestry

"Ancestry is one's family or ethnic descent."

What is your ancestry?_____

Have you explored your ancestry?_____

Are you curious about your ancestry?_____

How do you feel about your ancestry?_____

Are you proud of your ancestry? Why?_____

Write your thoughts here_____

Heritage

"Heritage is what we have inherited from the past, to value and enjoy in the present and to preserve and pass on to future generations."[51]

Heritage is "the background from which one comes from. An example of heritage is a German ancestry. An example of heritage is money left to a child in his parent's will.

Knowing your heritage may help you understand why you are the way you are.

Are you aware of your heritage?_____

Do you understand your heritage?_____

Who can you talk to about your heritage?_____

Heritage is important to me because_____

---

[51] "What is Heritage?" The Heritage Council, accessed January 27, 2023, https://www.heritagecouncil.ie/what-is-heritage#:~:text=Our%20heritage%20is%20what%20we,in%20museums%2C%20artefacts%20and%20archives.

Daily Positive Affirmations

Here are ten suggestions for daily positive affirmation that you may want to practice and put into action.

1. I will avoid negative thoughts.
2. I will think before I act.
3. I will respect myself.
4. I will respect the authority of my parents and my teachers.
5. I have great potential.
6. I will accomplish my goals.
7. I believe in myself.
8. I believe I can make positive change in my life.
9. I want to build people up. I do not want to tear people down.
10. I want to make a positive contribution to my life, family, and community.

List positive affirmation statements that you want to own.

1.

2.

3.

4.

5.

6.

7.

8.

9.

10.

Personal Hygiene

"Personal hygiene includes: cleaning your body every day, washing your hands with soap after going to the toilet, brushing your teeth twice a day, covering your mouth and nose with a tissue (or your sleeve) when sneezing or coughing."[52]

Is personal hygiene important to you?_____

Do you exercise good personal hygiene every day?_____

Do you neglect to care for your body?_____

How do you deal with others who may be offensive because of lack of good hygiene?

_____

[52] "What is personal hygiene?" Health Direct, accessed February 20, 2023, https://www.healthdirect.gov.au/personal-hygiene.

Image

"Image is the impression that a person presents to the public."

How important is your image to others?_____

Are you content with how you present yourself to others?_____

What would you like to change about your image?_____

How would you define how you present yourself to others?_____

_____

_____

_____

_____

_____

_____

_____

_____

_____

_____

Thoughts Chart

My Positive Thoughts My   Negative Thoughts

What do I want to change about my negative thinking?_____

How can I restructure my negative thoughts to more positive ones?_____

Think about the blessings in your life.

List the blessings in your life.

1.

2.

3.

4.

5.

6.

7.

_____

_____

_____

_____

_____

_____

Do You Value Family?

In what ways do you value family?

_____

_____

_____

How important are your family members to you?

The Impossible Dream

The impossible dream "is a highly desirable yet seemingly unattainable goal or aspiration."[53]

What seems impossible for you?_____

Do you feel stuck in fulfilling your dreams?_____

What is preventing you from fulfilling your dreams?_____

List three dreams you desire for your life.

Who do you need to help you accomplish your dreams?_____

_____and_____

What barriers are you experiencing to meeting your goals?_____

_____and_____

It's never too late to dream and make your dreams come true.

---

[53] Josh Quigley, "The Biggest Day So Far," LinkedIn post, 2020, https://uk.linkedin.com/posts/joshquigley2026_chooselife-activity-6549370613801209856-9aQE?trk=public_profile_like_view.

Value of Relationships

Do you value relationships?

How do you value relationships/friendships?

Relationship Circle

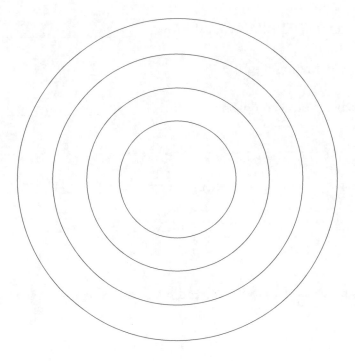

Who are the most important people in your life?_____

_____   _____

_____   _____

_____   _____

_____

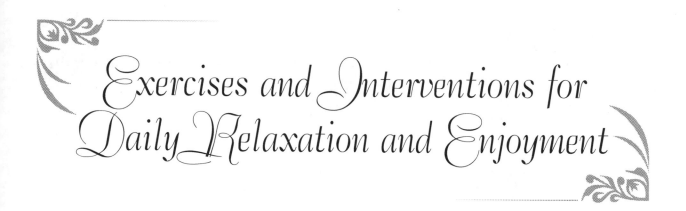

Exercises and Interventions for Daily Relaxation and Enjoyment

Practice Relaxation

Deep breathing sends a message to the brain to calm down.

Find time for you, take a few deep breaths in, and exhale out for your physical, mental, and emotional health.

Take a brief walk in the morning and, when possible, one in the evening. It helps with your overall health and helps you to sleep well.

If you have a pet, walking your pet in the morning and evening gives you good reason to take a walk and motivates you to walk even when you don't want to.

Listen to your favorite music daily. What kind of music do you like?_____

Music is calming, inspiring, and beneficial to your well-being.

Make time to get a massage. Treat yourself to something that is good for you physically, mentally, and emotionally. Find time to take a relaxing, uninterrupted bubble bath.

Where is your secret place to escape to in your mind?_____

Maybe on a beach? Close your eyes and imagine you are there.

Consequences

The consequences of our actions and behaviors

Everything in this life begins with two things: our thoughts and our words. Our thoughts determine our feelings and our feelings determine our actions. In other words, what we think about causes us to say what we are thinking and results in what action we take. We must stop and think about what actions we take for our own lives and the actions we take in the lives of others.

"There are consequences to our actions. Consequences can be positive or negative. Positive consequences reinforce behavior and make it more likely to happen again. Negative consequences make behavior less likely to happen again. Everything we think and say and do has consequences for ourselves and for others. There are consequences for our actions."

Have you experienced negative consequences for your actions?

Place your thoughts here.

_____

_____

_____

_____

_____

_____

_____

_____

Prayer

"Prayer is a solemn request for help or expression of thanks addressed to God or an object of worship or prayer can be seen as a conversation or relationship with God."

Prayer is a choice based on your belief system.

Do you use prayer as a strategy for change?_____

There is a popular statement that "prayer changes things."

Have you found that prayer works in your life?_____

Have you made a commitment to prayer?_____

Have you found that prayer works in your life?_____

What would you like to change about your prayer life?_____

What would you like to change about the path you are on?_____

Your thoughts_____

_____

_____

_____

_____

_____

_____

_____

Meditation

"Meditation is a practice in which an individual uses a technique—such as mindfulness, or focusing the mind on a particular object, thought, or activity—to train attention and awareness, and achieve a mentally clear and emotionally calm and stable state."[54]

Have you tried meditating?_____

Is meditating something you would like to experience?_____

Would you like to be calm in adverse situations?_____Meditating can help you focus.

Do you feel stable, focused, and calm more often than not?_____

Check out this website for more information on mindfulness: www.mindfulness.com

_____

_____

_____

_____

_____

_____

_____

_____

54   Wikipedia.com, s.v. "Meditation," accessed January 27, 2023, https://en.wikipedia.org/wiki/Meditation#:
      ~:text=Meditation%20is%20a%20practice%20in,emotionally%20calm%20and%20stable%20state.

Wellness

Wellness is "the state of being in good health, especially as an actively pursued goal."[55]

"Wellness is commonly viewed as having seven dimensions: mental, physical, social, financial, spiritual, environmental, and vocational. These dimensions are interdependent of each other. When one dimension of our well-being is out of balance, the other dimensions are affected."[56]

Why is wellness important you?_____

Have you had setbacks to balancing your overall health?_____

How can you improve your overall health?_____

Have you sought out help to improve your overall wellness?_____

Have you given your wellness much thought?_____

[55] Merriam-Webster.com, s.v. "wellness," accessed January 27, 2023, https://www.merriam-webster.com/dictionary/wellness.

[56] "Seven Dimensions of Wellness," Laurier, accessed January 27, 2023, https://students.wlu.ca/wellness-and-recreation/health-and-wellness/wellness-education/dimensions.html#:~:text=Wellness%20is%20commonly%20viewed%20as,the%20other%20dimensions%20are%20affected.

What works?

Let's think about what works for you.

Let's list what works. Pick a category to focus on, for example, the topic of respect.

1.

2.

3.

4.

What does not work?

Let's think about what does not work for you. List what does not work for you. Pick a topic for discussion, for example, disrespect.

What does not work?

1.

2.

3.

4.

Changing

First, having a desire and recognizing the need to change is paramount to changing. We all want to be our best selves. We all have areas in our lives that needs improvement. Changing is challenging. We have to want to change and we have to want to try something different. We have to push ourselves to become better individuals despite generational patterns and years of doing things the same way. Changing is evolving, growing, maturing; it can be like a metamorphosis experience that enables one to thrive. You can change for the better.

Your thoughts_____

_____

Transformation

"Human Transformation is an internal shift that brings us in alignment with our highest potential. It is the heart of every major aspect of our lives. It affects how we see and relate to the world and how we understand our place in it."[57]

It's up to you. We have been taught about metamorphosis. We have learned about how a caterpillar transforms into a butterfly. This may seem like a complex process but the outcome is beautiful and spectacular.

Your thoughts_____

_____

---

[57] Allaya Cooks-Campbell, "Becoming more you: What it means to transform as a human," BetterUp, posted January 20, 2022, https://www.betterup.com/blog/human-transformation.

Think about the blessings in your life.

List some of your blessings.

1.

2.

3.

4.

5.

6.

7.

8.

9.

10.

Action Plan for Change

That's Not Who I Am

What change will I make?   When will I do it?

Seek Professional Help

Seeking professional help is to request, pursue, or endeavor to obtain treatment or counseling from a psychologist or psychiatrist.

If you find that you have the inability to cope and your habits interfere with your daily routine, it's time to get help.

You can get referrals from your family doctor, clergy, or local mental health clinic.

Seeking professional help will give you the coping tools and strategies you need. You will be able to navigate challenging situations with a greater degree of awareness.

Closing

That's Not Who I Am

Take your time and work in this workbook. You will see areas of your life that you are satisfied with and you will see areas of your life where you want to make changes for your betterment and the betterment of others. Let's work on ourselves as we would work on our homes or cars or careers. We need an overhaul at least once a year. You want to go to the next level to do a paradigm shift in your life as you develop true satisfaction with yourself.

Remember, introspection can bring about positive change.

There are no limitations to how far we can rise to become who we want to be. Self-evaluation is always a good way to look at ourselves to see where we need to change. We do not want to say *That's Not Who I Am*, but keep making the same mistakes or demonstrating inappropriate, immature behaviors that harm ourselves, others, and the next generation that is watching us.

I can do all things through Christ that strengthened me. (Philippians 4:13)

Bibliography

"Accomplishing Forgiveness." Career Planning & Counseling Services, Piedmont Technical College. Accessed January 27, 2023. https://www.ptc.edu/sites/default/files/documents/student_services/accomplishing_forgiveness_with_footer_logo.pdf.

"All About Respect." Kidshelpline. Last updated October 17, 2017. https://kidshelpline.com.au/teens/issues/all-about-respect#:~:text=Respect%20means%20that%20you%20accept,it%20is%20something%20you%20learn.

Arscott, Sarah. "What is Love?" Medium. Posted July 13, 2020. https://medium.com/fearless-she-wrote/what-is-love-7695a6f9b23f.

Cooks-Campbell, Allaya. "Becoming more you: What it means to transform as a human." BetterUp. Posted January 20, 2022. https://www.betterup.com/blog/human-transformation.

Dahunsi, Lanre. "Quotes on Self-Awareness." Lanre Dahunsi. Posted June 20, 2021. https://lanredahunsi.com/quotes-on-self-awareness/.

DeAngelis, Tori. "In search of cultural competence." *Monitor on Psychology* 46, no. 3 (March 1, 2015): 64. https://www.apa.org/monitor/2015/03/cultural-competence.

DPS Staff. "10 Ways to Practice Positive Self-Talk." Delaware Psychological Associates. Posted April 23, 2021. https://www.delawarepsychologicalservices.com/post/10-ways-to-practice-positive-self-talk.

"Environmental factors that contribute to child vulnerability." OECDLibrary. Accessed January 27, 2023. https://www.oecd-ilibrary.org/sites/6a006a25-en/index.html?itemId=/content/component/6a006a25-en.

Gale, Cheryl. "Negative Self Talk—What is it and why does it matter?" Proactive Health + Movement. Accessed January 26, 2023. https://www.proactivehm.com.au/negative-self-talk-what-is-it-and-why-does-it-matter/#:~:text=Negative%20self%2Dtalk%20is%20any,your%20ability%20to%20do%20so.

"Gun Violence." American Public Health Association. Accessed February 16, 2023. https://www.apha.org/topics-and-issues/gun-violence.

"How to Use Self-Talk to Improve Performance." PsychCentral. Accessed January 26, 2023. https://psychcentral.com/blog/how-to-use-self-talk-to-improve-performance#1.

Jabbari, Bahareh and Audra S. Rouster. "Family Dynamics." *StatPearls* [Internet]. Treasure Island, FL: StatPearls Publishing, 2022.

Jabbour, Ralph. "The Importance of Cultivating Self-Discipline." Entrepreneur. Posted November 29, 2017. https://www.entrepreneur.com/en-ae/growth-strategies/the-importance-of-cultivating-self-discipline/305350#:~:text=Self%2Ddiscipline%2C%20by%20definition%2C,achieve%2C%20and%20dreams%20to%20chase.

Klein, Parker. "2 Different Types of Patience." Medium. Posted January 22, 2022. https://medium.com/twosapp/2-different-types-of-patience-2cd39201ef2b.

LaMorte, Wayne W. "What is Culture?" Boston University School of Public Health. Last modified May 3, 2016. https://sphweb.bumc.bu.edu/otlt/mph-modules/PH/CulturalAwareness/CulturalAwareness2.html#:~:text=Culture%20can%20be%20defined%20as,%2C%20religion%2C%20rituals%2C%20art.

Leoni, Julie. "Responsibility, control and power." Julie Leoni. Posted February 21, 2015. https://www.julieleoni.com/blog/relationships-and-family/responsibility-control-and-power/#:~:text=Responsibility%20is%20defined%20as%20'the,or%20to%20blame%20for%20something.

MacCammon, Gordon. "Cyberbullying and its Complications in Policy." Sienna College. Posted November 2017. https://www.siena.edu/files/resources/cyber-bullying-brief.pdf.

"Managing Stress." Center for Health Advocacy & Wellness. Florida State University. Accessed January 23, 2023. https://chaw.fsu.edu/topics/wellness/managing-stress#:~:text=Stress%20is%20the%20state%20of,also%20be%20emotional%20or%20behavioral.

McGough, Matt, Krutika Amin, Nirmita Panchal, and Cynthia Cox. "Child and Teen Firearm Mortality in the U.S. and Peer Countries." KFF. Posted July 8, 2022. https://www.kff.org/global-health-policy/issue-brief/child-and-teen-firearm-mortality-in-the-u-s-and-peer-countries/.

Morris, Susan York. "What Are the Benefits of Self-Talk?" Healthline. Last updated December 19, 2016. https://www.healthline.com/health/mental-health/self-talk.

Philo, S.W., M.F. Richie, and M.J. Kaas. "Inappropriate Sexual Behavior." *Journal of Gerontological Nursing* 22, no. 1 (November 1996): 17-22. https://doi.org/10.3928/0098-9134-19961101-07.

Quigley, Josh. "The Biggest Day So Far." LinkedIn post. 2020. https://uk.linkedin.com/posts/joshquigley2026_chooselife-activity-6549370613801209856-9aQE?trk=public_profile_like_view.

"Self-talk." Health Direct. Accessed January 26, 2023. https://www.healthdirect.gov.au/self-talk.

"Seven Dimensions of Wellness." Laurier. Accessed January 27, 2023. https://students.wlu.ca/wellness-and-recreation/health-and-wellness/wellness-education/dimensions.html#:~:text=Wellness%20is%20commonly%20viewed%20as,the%20other%20dimensions%20are%20affected.

"Substance Abuse Among College Students." Affordable Colleges. Accessed January 27, 2023. https://www.affordablecollegesonline.org/college-resource-center/substance-abuse-in-college/.

Wallace, Brianna. "The object of a person's ambition or effort; an aim or desired result. Goals." Alexander Muss High School in Israel. Posted June 26, 2019. https://www.amhsi.org/amhsi-blog/amhsi-blog/2019/06/26/the-object-of-a-person's-ambition-or-effort-an-aim-or-desired-result.-goals.

Waters, Shonna "Family dynamics can lift you up (or drag you down)." BetterUp. Posted December 10, 2021. https://www.betterup.com/blog/family-dynamics#:~:text=Family%20dynamics%20are%20how%20members,%2Dbeing%2C%20and%20work%20relationships.

"What is forgiveness?" Greater Good Magazine. Accessed February 16, 2023. https://greatergood.berkeley.edu/topic/forgiveness/definition#:~:text=I%20Cultivate%20It%3F-,What%20Is%20Forgiveness%3F,they%20actually%20deserve%20your%20forgiveness.

"What is Happiness?" Verywellmind. Last updated November 7, 2022. https://www.verywellmind.com/what-is-happiness-4869755.

"What is Heritage?" The Heritage Council. Accessed January 27, 2023. https://www.heritagecouncil.ie/what-is-heritage#:~:text=Our%20heritage%20is%20what%20we,in%20museums%2C%20artefacts%20and%20archives.

"What is Peer Pressure?" Study.com. Accessed January 27, 2023. https://study.com/academy/lesson/what-is-peer-pressure-definition-lesson-quiz.html.

"What is personal hygiene?" Health Direct. Accessed February 20, 2023. https://www.healthdirect.gov.au/personal-hygiene.

"What is Trust?" BrandonCoussensLMFT. Accessed January 26, 2023. https://brandoncoussens lmft.com/what-is-trust/#:~:text =Trust%20is%20a%20firm%20belief,truth%20of%20 someone%20or%20something.

"Vol 3: Self." The Kindred Voice. Accessed January 26, 2023. https://www.thekindredvoice. com/shop/p/vol3self#:~:text=Self%3A%20a%20person's%20essential%20being,of%20 introspection%20or%20reflexive%20action.

Printed in the United States
by Baker & Taylor Publisher Services